SPIRITUAL GROWTH

BIBLE STUDY

SPIRITUAL GROWTH

DAY 1

THE STARTING

Main Point: Spiritual wisdom begins with deep reverence for God.

Therefore, my dear friends, as you have always obeyed—not only in my presence, but now much more in my absence—continue to work out your salvation with fear and trembling, for it is God who works in you to will and to act in order to fulfill his good purpose.

—*Philippians 2:12-13*

TODAY'S QUESTION: *IN WHAT WAYS DO YOU THINK OBEDIENCE IS A PART OF HAVING A DEEP REVERENCE FOR GOD?*

READ ALSO: PROVERBS 1:7

ADDITIONAL READING

I JOHN 2:3-6

By this we know that we have come to know Him, if we keep His commandments. The one who says, "I have come to know Him," and does not keep His commandments, is a liar, and the truth is not in him; but whoever keeps His word, in him the love of God has truly been perfected. By this we know that we are in Him: the one who says he abides in Him ought himself to walk in the same manner as He walked." (NASB)

2 JOHN 1:6-9

And this is love, that we walk according to His commandments. This is the commandment, just as you have heard from the beginning, that you should walk in it.

For many deceivers have gone out into the world, those who do not acknowledge Jesus Christ as coming in the flesh. This is the deceiver and the antichrist. Watch yourselves, that you do not lose what we have accomplished, but that you may receive a full reward. Anyone who goes too far and does not abide in the teaching of Christ, does not have God; the one who abides in the teaching, he has both the Father and the Son." (NASB)

DAY 2

THE #1

Main point: Nothing is more important than loving God more fully and then loving others.

Trust in the Lord with all your heart

    and lean not on your own understanding;

in all your ways submit to him,

    and he will make your paths straight.

—*Proverbs 3:5-6*

TODAY'S QUESTION: WHAT CAN THESE VERSES TEACH US ABOUT THE IMPORTANCE OF LOVING GOD?

READ ALSO: MATTEW 22:34-40

ADDITIONAL READING

I JOHN 5:1-12

Everyone who believes that Jesus is the Messiah has been born from God. Everyone who loves the Father also loves his children. We know that we love God's children when we love God by obeying his commandments. To love God means that we obey his commandments. Obeying his commandments isn't difficult because everyone who has been born from God has won the victory over the world. Our faith is what wins the victory over the world. Who wins the victory over the world? Isn't it the person who believes that Jesus is the Son of God?

This Son of God is Jesus Christ, who came by water and blood. He didn't come with water only, but with water and with blood. The Spirit is the one who verifies this, because the Spirit is the truth. There are three witnesses: the Spirit, the water, and the blood. These three witnesses agree.

We accept human testimony. God's testimony is greater because it is the testimony that he has given about his Son. Those who believe in the Son of God have the testimony of God in them. Those who don't believe God have made God a liar. They haven't believed the testimony that God has given about his Son.

This is the testimony: God has given us eternal life, and this life is found in his Son. The person who has the Son has this life. The person who doesn't have the Son of God doesn't have this life." (GWT)

DAY 3

GROUND RULES CARVED IN

Main Point: The Ten Commandments remain standards of behavior that please God.

And God spoke all these words:

"I am the Lord your God, who brought you out of Egypt, out of the land of slavery.

You shall have no other gods before me.

You shall not make for yourself an image in the form of anything in heaven above or on the earth beneath or in the waters below."

—*Exodus 20:1-4*

TODAY'S QUESTION: WHAT CAN WE LEARN ABOUT GOD FROM THESE VERSES?

READ ALSO: DEUTERONOMY 11:16

ADDITIONAL READING

LEVITICUS 26:1-13

"You shall not make idols for yourselves or erect an image or pillar, and you shall not set up a figured stone in your land to bow down to it, for I am the Lord your God. You shall keep my Sabbaths and reverence my sanctuary: I am the Lord.

"If you walk in my statutes and observe my commandments and do them, then I will give you your rains in their season, and the land shall yield its increase, and the trees of the field shall yield their fruit. Your threshing shall last to the time of the grape harvest, and the grape harvest shall last to the time for sowing. And you shall eat your bread to the full and dwell in your land securely. I will give peace in the land, and you shall lie down, and none shall make you afraid. And I will remove harmful beasts from the land, and the sword shall not go through your land. You shall chase your enemies, and they shall fall before you by the sword. Five of you shall chase a hundred, and a hundred of you shall chase ten thousand, and your enemies shall fall before you by the sword. I will turn to you and make you fruitful and multiply you and will confirm my covenant with you. You shall eat old store long kept, and you shall clear out the old to make way for the new. I will make my dwelling among you, and my soul shall not abhor you. And I will walk among you and will be your God, and you shall be my people. I am the Lord your God, who brought you out of the land of Egypt, that you should not be their slaves. And I have broken the bars of your yoke and made you walk erect. (ESV)

DAY 4

WORTH THE WEIGHT

*Main Point: Commitment to Christ requires both
a new commitment and change of priorities.*

Then Jesus said to his disciples, "Whoever wants
to be my disciple must deny themselves and take
up their cross and follow me. For whoever wants
to save their life will lose it, but whoever loses their
life for me will find it. What good will it be for
someone to gain the whole world, yet forfeit their
soul? Or what can anyone give in exchange for their
soul? For the Son of Man is going to come in his
Father's glory with his angels, and then he will reward each person according to what they have done.

—*Matthew 16:24-27*

TODAY'S QUESTION: WHAT DO YOU THINK
IT MEANS TO BE A DISCIPLE OF JESUS?

READ ALSO: MATTHEW 11:28-30

ADDITIONAL READING

DANIEL 3:1-30

King Nebuchadnezzar made a golden statue whose height was sixty cubits and whose width was six cubits; he set it up on the plain of Dura in the province of Babylon. Then King Nebuchadnezzar sent for the satraps, the prefects, and the governors, the counselors, the treasurers, the justices, the magistrates, and all the officials of the provinces to assemble and come to the dedication of the statue that King Nebuchadnezzar had set up. So the satraps, the prefects, and the governors, the counselors, the treasurers, the justices, the magistrates, and all the officials of the provinces, assembled for the dedication of the statue that King Nebuchadnezzar had set up. When they were standing before the statue that Nebuchadnezzar had set up, the herald proclaimed aloud, "You are commanded, O peoples, nations, and languages, that when you hear the sound of the horn, pipe, lyre, trigon, harp, drum, and entire musical ensemble, you are to fall down and worship the golden statue that King Nebuchadnezzar has set up. Whoever does not fall down and worship shall immediately be thrown into a furnace of blazing fire." Therefore, as soon as all the peoples heard the sound of the horn, pipe, lyre, trigon, harp, drum, and entire musical ensemble, all the peoples, nations, and languages fell down and worshiped the golden statue that King Nebuchadnezzar had set up.

Accordingly, at this time certain Chaldeans came forward and denounced the Jews. They said to King Nebuchadnezzar, "O king, live forever! You, O king, have made a decree, that everyone who hears the sound of the horn, pipe, lyre, trigon, harp, drum, and entire musical ensemble, shall fall down and worship the golden statue, and whoever does not fall down and worship shall be thrown into a furnace of blazing fire. There are certain Jews whom you have appointed over the affairs of the province of Babylon: Shadrach, Meshach, and Abednego. These pay no heed to you, O King. They do not serve your gods and they do not worship the golden statue that you have set up."

Then Nebuchadnezzar in furious rage commanded that Shadrach, Meshach, and Abednego be brought in; so they brought those men before the king. Nebuchadnezzar said to them, "Is it true, O Shadrach, Meshach, and Abednego, that you do not serve my gods and you do not worship the golden statue that I have set up? Now if you are ready when you hear the sound of the horn, pipe, lyre, trigon, harp, drum, and entire musical ensemble to fall down and worship the statue that I have made, well and good. But if you do not worship, you shall immediately be thrown into a furnace of blazing fire, and who is the god that will deliver you out of my hands?"

Shadrach, Meshach, and Abednego answered the king, "O Nebuchadnezzar, we have no need to present a defense to you in this matter. If our God whom we serve is able to deliver us from the furnace of blazing fire and out of your hand, O king, let him deliver us. But if not, be it known to you, O king, that we will not serve your gods and we will not worship the golden statue that you have set up."

Then Nebuchadnezzar was so filled with rage against Shadrach, Meshach, and Abednego that his face was distorted. He ordered the furnace heated up seven times more than was customary, and ordered some of the strongest guards in his army to bind Shadrach, Meshach, and Abednego and to throw them into the furnace of blazing fire. So the men were bound, still wearing their tunics, their trousers, their hats, and their other garments, and they were thrown into the furnace of blazing fire. Because the king's command was urgent and the furnace was so overheated, the raging flames killed the men who lifted Shadrach, Meshach, and Abednego. But the three men, Shadrach, Meshach, and Abednego, fell down, bound, into the furnace of blazing fire.

Then King Nebuchadnezzar was astonished and rose up quickly. He said to his counselors, "Was it not three men that we threw bound into the fire?" They answered the king, "True, O king." He replied, "But I see four men unbound, walking in the middle of the fire, and they are not hurt; and the fourth has the appearance of a god." Nebuchadnezzar then approached the door of the furnace of blazing fire and said, "Shadrach, Meshach, and Abednego, servants of the Most High God, come out! Come here!" So Shadrach, Meshach, and Abednego came out from the fire. And the satraps, the prefects, the governors, and the king's counselors gathered together and saw that the fire had not had any power over the bodies of those men; the hair of their heads was not singed, their tunics were not harmed, and not even the smell of fire came from them. Nebuchadnezzar said, "Blessed be the God of Shadrach, Meshach, and Abednego, who has sent his angel and delivered his servants who trusted in him. They disobeyed the king's command and yielded up their bodies rather than serve and worship any god except their own God. Therefore I make a decree: Any people, nation, or language that utters blasphemy against the God of Shadrach, Meshach, and Abednego shall be torn limb from limb, and their houses laid in ruins; for there is no other god who is able to deliver in this way." Then the king promoted Shadrach, Meshach, and Abednego in the province of Babylon." (NRSV)

NEBUCHADNEZZAR SAID,
"BLESSED BE THE GOD OF SHADRACH,
MESHACH, AND ABEDNEGO, WHO HAS
SENT HIS ANGEL AND DELIVERED HIS
SERVANTS WHO TRUSTED IN HIM."

DAY 5

UNUSUAL DEFINITIONS OF HAPPINESS

*Main Point: Jesus' standards for personal fulfill-
ment are quite different from cultural standards.*

Blessed are the peacemakers,
    for they will be called children of God.
Blessed are those who are persecuted because of
    righteousness,
    for theirs is the kingdom of heaven.

Blessed are you when people insult you, persecute
you and falsely say all kinds of evil against you
because of me. Rejoice and be glad, because great
is your reward in heaven, for in the same way they
persecuted the prophets who were before you.

—Matthew 5:9-12

*TODAY'S QUESTION: IN WHAT WAYS ARE
YOU INSPIRED BY THESE VERSES?*

READ ALSO: PSALM 47:1

ADDITIONAL READING

2 PETER 1:3-8

God's divine power has given us everything we need for life and for godliness. This power was given to us through knowledge of the one who called us by his own glory and integrity. Through his glory and integrity he has given us his promises that are of the highest value. Through these promises you will share in the divine nature because you have escaped the corruption that sinful desires cause in the world.

Because of this, make every effort to add integrity to your faith; and to integrity add knowledge; to knowledge add self-control; to self-control add endurance; to endurance add godliness; to godliness add Christian affection; and to Christian affection add love. If you have these qualities and they are increasing, it demonstrates that your knowledge about our Lord Jesus Christ is living and productive. (GWT)

JEREMIAH 11 : 3 – 5

Tell them that this is what the LORD, the God
of Israel, says: "Cursed is the man who does not
obey the terms of this covenant –the terms I commanded your forefathers when I brought them
out of Egypt, out of the iron-smelting furnace."
I said, "Obey me and do everything I command
you, and you will be my people, and I will be your
God. Then I will fulfill the oath I swore to your
forefathers, to give them a land flowing with milk
and honey " – the land you possess today." (NIV)

DAY 6

WHICH TIME IS IT?

Main Point: Specific circumstances should be considered before determining the best response.

There is a time for everything,

and a season for every activity under the heavens:

a time to be born and a time to die,

a time to plant and a time to uproot,

a time to kill and a time to heal,

a time to tear down and a time to build,

a time to weep and a time to laugh,

a time to mourn and a time to dance.

—*Ecclesiastes 3:1-4*

TODAY'S QUESTION: IN WHAT WAYS ARE YOU ENCOURAGED BY THESE VERSES?

READ ALSO: PSALM 90:12

ADDITIONAL READING

JOB 14:1-17

"Man, born of woman,

lives but a few days, and they are full of trouble.

He grows up like a flower and then withers away;

he flees like a shadow, and does not remain.

Do you fix your eye on such a one?

And do you bring me before you for judgment?

Who can make a clean thing come from an unclean?

No one!

Since man's days are determined,

the number of his months is under your control;

you have set his limit and he cannot pass it.

Look away from him and let him desist,

until he fulfills his time like a hired man.

"But there is hope for a tree:

If it is cut down, it will sprout again,

and its new shoots will not fail.

Although its roots may grow old in the ground

and its stump begins to die in the soil,

at the scent of water it will flourish

and put forth shoots like a new plant.

But man dies and is powerless;

he expires—and where is he?

As water disappears from the sea,

or a river drains away and dries up,

so man lies down and does not rise;

until the heavens are no more,

they will not awake

nor arise from their sleep.

"O that you would hide me in Sheol,

and conceal me till your anger has passed!

O that you would set me a time

and then remember me!

If a man dies, will he live again?

All the days of my hard service I will wait

until my release comes.

You will call and I—I will answer you;

you will long for the creature you have made.

"Surely now you count my steps;

then you would not mark my sin.

My offenses would be sealed up in a bag;

you would cover over my sin. (NET Bible)

DAY 7

SUIT UP!

*Main Point: God provides "armor" for
our difficult spiritual struggles.*

Stand firm then, with the belt of truth buckled
around your waist, with the breastplate of righteousness in place, and with your feet fitted with the
readiness that comes from the gospel of peace. In
addition to all this, take up the shield of faith, with
which you can extinguish all the flaming arrows
of the evil one. Take the helmet of salvation and
the sword of the Spirit, which is the word of God.

—Ephesians 6:14-17

*TODAY'S QUESTION: WHERE HAVE YOU FOUND
STRENGTH IN YOUR FIGHT AGAINST SPIRITUAL STRUGGLES?*

READ ALSO: JAMES 4:7

ADDITIONAL READING

PHILIPPIANS 3:7-11

But whatever things were gain to me, those things I have counted as loss for the sake of Christ. More than that, I count all things to be loss in view of the surpassing value of knowing Christ Jesus my Lord, for whom I have suffered the loss of all things, and count them but rubbish so that I may gain Christ, and may be found in Him, not having a righteousness of my own derived from the Law, but that which is through faith in Christ, the righteousness which comes from God on the basis of faith, that I may know Him and the power of His resurrection and the fellowship of His sufferings, being conformed to His death; in order that I may attain to the resurrection from the dead." (NASB)

I THESSALONIANS 5:8-11

But since we are of the day, let us be sober, having put on the breastplate of faith and love, and as a helmet, the hope of salvation. For God has not destined us for wrath, but for obtaining salvation through our

Lord Jesus Christ, who died for us, so that whether we are awake or asleep, we will live together with Him. Therefore encourage one another and build up one another, just as you also are doing." (NASB)

I TIMOTHY 6:11-12

But flee from these things, you man of God, and pursue righteousness, godliness, faith, love, perseverance and gentleness. Fight the good fight of faith; take hold of the eternal life to which you were called, and you made the good confession in the presence of many witnesses." (NASB)

DAY 8

A MUCH-OVERLOOKED QUALITY

Main Point: Believers are challenged to acknowledge and emulate the humility of Christ.

Therefore God exalted him to the highest place
   and gave him the name that is above every name,
that at the name of Jesus every knee should bow,
   in heaven and on earth and under the earth,
   and every tongue acknowledge that Jesus Christ
   is Lord,
   to the glory of God the Father.

—Philippians 2:9-11

TODAY'S QUESTION: WHAT CAN THESE VERSES TEACH US ABOUT JESUS?

READ ALSO: 1 PETER 5:5-7

ADDITIONAL READING

MARK 10:13-16

And they were bringing children to him that he might touch them, and the disciples rebuked them. But when Jesus saw it, he was indignant and said to them, "Let the children come to me; do not hinder them, for to such belongs the kingdom of God. Truly, I say to you, whoever does not receive the kingdom of God like a child shall not enter it." And he took them in his arms and blessed them, laying his hands on them. (ESV)

LUKE 17:5-6

One day the apostles said to the Lord, "We need more faith; tell us how to get it."

"Even if you had faith as small as a mustard seed," the Lord answered, "you could say to this mulberry tree, 'May God uproot you and throw you into the sea,' and it would obey you!" (NLT)

MATTHEW 21:16

And they said to him, "Do you hear what these are saying?" And Jesus said to them, "Yes; have you never read,

"'Out of the mouth of infants and nursing babies you have prepared praise?" (NIV)

ISAIAH 40:27-31

Why do you complain, Jacob? Why do you say, Israel, "My way is hidden from the LORD; my cause is disregarded by my God"? Do you not know? Have you not heard? The LORD is the everlasting God, the Creator of the ends of the earth. He will not grow tired or weary, and his understanding no one can fathom. He gives strength to the weary and increases the power of the weak. Even youths grow tired and weary, and young men stumble and fall; but those who hope in the LORD will renew their strength. They will soar on wings like eagles; they will run and not grow weary, they will walk and not be faint. (NIV)

DAY 9

SALT AND LIGHT

Main Point: As "salt" and "light," believers should influence their culture without being absorbed by it.

You are the salt of the earth. But if the salt loses its saltiness, how can it be made salty again? It is no longer good for anything, except to be thrown out and trampled underfoot.

You are the light of the world. A town built on a hill cannot be hidden. Neither do people light a lamp and put it under a bowl. Instead they put it on its stand, and it gives light to everyone in the house. In the same way, let your light shine before others, that they may see your good deeds and glorify your Father in heaven.

—*Matthew 5:13-16*

TODAY'S QUESTION: WHAT DO YOU THINK
IT LOOKS LIKE TO BE SALT AND LIGHT?

READ ALSO: PHILIPPIANS 2:15

ADDITIONAL READING

ACTS 5:28-32

"We gave you strict orders not to teach in this name," he said. "Yet you have filled Jerusalem with your teaching and are determined to make us guilty of this man's blood."

Peter and the other apostles replied: "We must obey God rather than men! The God of our fathers raised Jesus from the dead--whom you had killed by hanging him on a tree. God exalted him to his own right hand as Prince and Savior that he might give repentance and forgiveness of sins to Israel. We are witnesses of these things, and so is the Holy Spirit, whom God has given to those who obey him." (NIV)

PSALM 1:1-6

Blessed is the person who does not

follow the advice of wicked people,

take the path of sinners,

or join the company of mockers.

Rather, he delights in the teachings of the Lord

and reflects on his teachings day and night.

He is like a tree planted beside streams—

a tree that produces fruit in season

and whose leaves do not wither. He
succeeds in everything he does.

Wicked people are not like that.

Instead, they are like husks that
the wind blows away.

That is why wicked people will not
be able to stand in the judgment

and sinners will not be able to stand
where righteous people gather.

The Lord knows the way of righteous people,

but the way of wicked people will end. (GWT)

DAY 10

YOU HEARD IT WRONG

Main Point: Jesus clarified [and corrected] several longstanding religious traditions.

But I tell you, love your enemies and pray for those who persecute you, that you may be children of your Father in heaven. He causes his sun to rise on the evil and the good, and sends rain on the righteous and the unrighteous. If you love those who love you, what reward will you get? Are not even the tax collectors doing that? And if you greet only your own people, what are you doing more than others? Do not even pagans do that? Be perfect, therefore, as your heavenly Father is perfect.

—*Matthew 5:44-48*

TODAY'S QUESTION: WHY DO YOU THINK LOVING OTHERS IS IMPORTANT WHEN FOLLOWING JESUS?

READ ALSO: PROVERBS 19:11

ADDITIONAL READING

PHILIPPIANS 1:27

Only conduct yourselves in a manner worthy of the gospel of Christ, so that whether I come and see you or remain absent, I will hear of you that you are standing firm in one spirit, with one mind striving together for the faith of the gospel; (NASB)

EPHESIANS 5:1

Therefore be imitators of God, as beloved children; (NASB)

1 PETER 1:13-22

Therefore, prepare your minds for action, keep sober in spirit, fix your hope completely on the grace to be brought to you at the revelation of Jesus Christ. As obedient children, do not be conformed to the former lusts which were yours in your ignorance, but like the Holy One who called you, be holy yourselves also in all your behavior; because it is written, "YOU SHALL BE HOLY, FOR I AM HOLY."

If you address as Father the One who impartially judges according to each one's work, conduct yourselves in fear during the time of your stay on earth; knowing that you were not redeemed with perishable things like silver or gold from your futile way of life inherited from your forefathers, but with precious blood, as of a lamb unblemished and spotless, the blood of Christ. For He was foreknown before the foundation of the world, but has appeared in these last times for the sake of you who through Him are believers in God, who raised Him from the dead and gave Him glory, so that your faith and hope are in God.

Since you have in obedience to the truth purified your souls for a sincere love of the brethren, fervently love one another from the heart.

DAY 11

SPIRITUAL DISCIPLINES: FOR GOD OR FOR SHOW?

Main Point: Believers should strive to avoid hypocrisy in spiritual commitment and growth.

"When you fast, do not look somber as the hypocrites do, for they disfigure their faces to show others they are fasting. Truly I tell you, they have received their reward in full. But when you fast, put oil on your head and wash your face, so that it will not be obvious to others that you are fasting, but only to your Father, who is unseen; and your Father, who sees what is done in secret, will reward you.

—Matthew 6:16-18

TODAY'S QUESTION: IN WHAT WAYS ARE YOU ENCOURAGED IN KNOWING THAT GOD SEES WHAT YOU DO?

READ ALSO: MATTHEW 6:4-6

ADDITIONAL READING

MATTHEW 23:13-36

"But woe to you, experts in the law and you Pharisees, hypocrites! You keep locking people out of the kingdom of heaven! For you neither enter nor permit those trying to enter to go in.

"Woe to you, experts in the law and you Pharisees, hypocrites! You cross land and sea to make one convert, and when you get one, you make him twice as much a child of hell as yourselves!

"Woe to you, blind guides, who say, 'Whoever swears by the temple is bound by nothing. But whoever swears by the gold of the temple is bound by the oath.' Blind fools! Which is greater, the gold or the temple that makes the gold sacred? And, 'Whoever swears by the altar is bound by nothing. But if anyone swears by the gift on it he is bound by the oath.' You are blind! For which is greater, the gift or the altar that makes the gift sacred? So whoever swears by the altar swears by it and by everything on it. And whoever swears by the temple swears by it and the one who dwells in it. And whoever swears by heaven swears by the throne of God and the one who sits on it.

"Woe to you, experts in the law and you Pharisees, hypocrites! You give a tenth of mint, dill, and cumin, yet you neglect what is more important in the law—justice, mercy, and faithfulness! You should have done these things without neglecting the others. Blind guides! You strain out a gnat yet swallow a camel!

"Woe to you, experts in the law and you Pharisees, hypocrites! You clean the outside of the cup and the dish, but inside they are full of greed and self-indulgence. Blind Pharisee! First clean the inside of the cup, so that the outside may become clean too!

"Woe to you, experts in the law and you Pharisees, hypocrites! You are like whitewashed tombs that look beautiful on the outside but inside are full of the bones of the dead and of everything unclean. In the same way, on the outside you look righteous to people, but inside you are full of hypocrisy and lawlessness.

"Woe to you, experts in the law and you Pharisees, hypocrites! You build tombs for the prophets and decorate the graves of the righteous. And you say, 'If we had lived in the days of our ancestors, we would not have participated with them in shedding the blood of the prophets.' By saying this you testify against yourselves that you are descendants of those who murdered the prophets. Fill up then the measure of your ancestors! You snakes, you offspring of vipers! How will you escape being condemned to hell?

"For this reason I am sending you prophets and wise men and experts in the law, some of whom you will kill and crucify, and some you will flog in your synagogues and pursue from town to town, so that on you will come all the righteous blood shed on earth, from the blood of righteous Abel to the blood of Zechariah son of Barachiah, whom you murdered between the temple and the altar. I tell you the truth, this generation will be held responsible for all these things!" (NET Bible)

DAY 12

DON'T WORRY ABOUT IT

*Main Point: We should trust God enough to
see us through our worrisome difficulties.*

Therefore I tell you, do not worry about your life,
what you will eat or drink; or about your body, what
you will wear. Is not life more than food, and the
body more than clothes? Look at the birds of the
air; they do not sow or reap or store away in barns,
and yet your heavenly Father feeds them. Are you
not much more valuable than they? Can any one
of you by worrying add a single hour to your life?

—*Matthew 6:25-27*

*TODAY'S QUESTION: IN WHAT WAYS ARE
YOU STRENGTHENED BY THESE VERSES?*

READ ALSO: PSALMS 55:22

ADDITIONAL READING

HEBREWS 10:19-25

Therefore, brothers, since we have confidence to enter the Most Holy Place by the blood of Jesus, by a new and living way opened for us through the curtain, that is, his body, and since we have a great priest over the house of God, let us draw near to God with a sincere heart in full assurance of faith, having our hearts sprinkled to cleanse us from a guilty conscience and having our bodies washed with pure water. Let us hold unswervingly to the hope we profess, for he who promised is faithful. And let us consider how we may spur one another on toward love and good deeds. Let us not give up meeting together, as some are in the habit of doing, but let us encourage one another--and all the more as you see the Day approaching." (NIV)

HEBREWS 4:16

Let us then approach God's throne of grace with confidence, so that we may receive mercy and find grace to help us in our time of need. (NIV)

LET US THEN APPROACH GOD'S
THRONE OF GRACE WITH CONFIDENCE.

DAY 13

CARING ENOUGH TO CORRECT

Main Point: God's discipline proves his love for us and should be welcomed.

And have you completely forgotten this
word of encouragement that addresses you
as a father addresses his son? It says,

"My son, do not make light of the Lord's discipline,
    and do not lose heart when he rebukes you,
because the Lord disciplines the one he loves,
    and he chastens everyone he accepts as his son."

Endure hardship as discipline; God is treating you as
his children. For what children are not disciplined
by their father? If you are not disciplined—and
everyone undergoes discipline—then you are not
legitimate, not true sons and daughters at all.

—*Hebrews 12:5-8*

TODAY'S QUESTION: *WHAT CAN WE LEARN
ABOUT GOD'S DISCIPLINE FROM THESE VERSES?*

READ ALSO: DEUTERONOMY 8:1-5

ADDITIONAL READING

Very truly, I tell you, the one who believes in me
will also do the works that I do and, in fact, will
do greater works than these, because I am going to
the Father. I will do whatever you ask in my name,
so that the Father may be glorified in the Son. If
in my name you ask me for anything, I will do it.

"If you love me, you will keep my commandments. And I will ask the Father, and he will
give you another Advocate, to be with you forever. This is the Spirit of truth, whom the world
cannot receive, because it neither sees him nor
knows him. You know him, because he abides
with you, and he will be in you. (NRSV)

JOHN 14:23-24

Jesus answered him, "Those who love me will
keep my word, and my Father will love them, and
we will come to them and make our home with
them. Whoever does not love me does not keep

my words; and the word that you hear is not mine,
but is from the Father who sent me. (NRSV)

EZEKIEL 5:7-8

Therefore this is what the Sovereign LORD says:
You have been more unruly than the nations around
you and have not followed my decrees or kept my
laws. You have not even conformed to the standards of the nations around you. 8)"Therefore this
is what the Sovereign LORD says: I myself am
against you, Jerusalem, and I will inflict punish-
ment on you in the sight of the nations (NIV)

DAY 14

OH, GOOD. I'M SUFFERING AGAIN

Main Point: If we realize that suffering has benefits, we can learn to better appreciate our trials.

Consider it pure joy, my brothers and sisters, whenever you face trials of many kinds, because you know that the testing of your faith produces perseverance. Let perseverance finish its work so that you may be mature and complete, not lacking anything. If any of you lacks wisdom, you should ask God, who gives generously to all without finding fault, and it will be given to you.

—James 1:2-5

TODAY'S QUESTION: *IN WHAT WAYS HAVE YOU FOUND STRENGTH IN YOUR TRIALS AND STRUGGLES?*

READ ALSO: ROMANS 5:1-5

ADDITIONAL READING

HEBREWS 11:1-40

What is faith? It is the confident assurance that what we hope for is going to happen. It is the evidence of things we cannot yet see. God gave his approval to people in days of old because of their faith.

By faith we understand that the entire universe was formed at God's command, that what we now see did not come from anything that can be seen.

It was by faith that Abel brought a more acceptable offering to God than Cain did. God accepted Abel's offering to show that he was a righteous man. And although Abel is long dead, he still speaks to us because of his faith.

It was by faith that Enoch was taken up to heaven without dying—"suddenly he disappeared because God took him." But before he was taken up, he was approved as pleasing to God. So, you see, it is impossible to please God without faith. Anyone who wants to come to him must believe that there is a God and that he rewards those who sincerely seek him.

It was by faith that Noah built an ark to save his family from the flood. He obeyed God, who warned him about something that had never happened before. By his faith he condemned the rest of the world and was made right in God's sight.

It was by faith that Abraham obeyed when God called him to leave home and go to another land that God would give him as his inheritance. He went without knowing where he was going. And even when he reached the land God promised him, he lived there by faith—for he was like a foreigner, living in a tent. And so did Isaac and Jacob, to whom God gave the same promise. Abraham did this because he was confidently looking forward to a city with eternal foundations, a city designed and built by God.

It was by faith that Sarah together with Abraham was able to have a child, even though they were too old and Sarah was barren. Abraham believed that God would keep his promise. And so a whole nation came from this one man, Abraham, who was too old to have any children—a nation with so many people that, like the stars of the sky and the sand on the seashore, there is no way to count them.

All these faithful ones died without receiving what God had promised them, but they saw it all from a distance and welcomed the promises of God. They agreed that they were no more than foreigners and nomads here on earth. And obviously people who talk like that are looking forward to a country they can call their own. If they had meant the country they came from, they would have found a way to go back. But they were looking for a better place, a heavenly homeland. That is why God is not ashamed to be called their God, for he has prepared a heavenly city for them.

It was by faith that Abraham offered Isaac as a sacrifice when God was testing him. Abraham, who had received God's promises, was ready to sacrifice his only son, Isaac, though God had promised him, "Isaac is the son through whom your descendants will be counted." Abraham assumed that if Isaac died, God was able to bring him back to life again. And in a sense, Abraham did receive his son back from the dead.

It was by faith that Isaac blessed his two sons, Jacob and Esau. He had confidence in what God was going to do in the future.

It was by faith that Jacob, when he was old and dying, blessed each of Joseph's sons and bowed in worship as he leaned on his staff.

And it was by faith that Joseph, when he was about to die, confidently spoke of God's bringing the people of Israel out of Egypt. He was so sure of it that he commanded them to carry his bones with them when they left!

It was by faith that Moses' parents hid him for three months. They saw that God had given them an unusual child, and they were not afraid of what the king might do.

It was by faith that Moses, when he grew up, refused to be treated as the son of Pharaoh's daughter. He chose to share the oppression of God's people instead of enjoying the fleeting pleasures of sin. He thought it was better to suffer for the sake of the Messiah than to own the treasures of Egypt, for he was looking ahead to the great reward that God would give him. It was by faith that Moses left the land of Egypt. He was not afraid of the king. Moses kept right on going because he kept his eyes on the one who is invisible. It was by faith that Moses commanded the people of Israel to keep the Passover and to sprinkle blood on the doorposts so that the angel of death would not kill their firstborn sons.

It was by faith that the people of Israel went right through the Red Sea as though they were on dry ground. But when the Egyptians followed, they were all drowned.

It was by faith that the people of Israel marched around Jericho seven days, and the walls came crashing down.

It was by faith that Rahab the prostitute did not die with all the others in her city who refused to obey God. For she had given a friendly welcome to the spies.

Well, how much more do I need to say? It would take too long to recount the stories of the faith of Gideon, Barak, Samson, Jephthah, David, Samuel, and all the prophets. By faith these people overthrew kingdoms, ruled with justice, and received what

God had promised them. They shut the mouths of lions, quenched the flames of fire, and escaped death by the edge of the sword. Their weakness was turned to strength. They became strong in battle and put whole armies to flight. Women received their loved ones back again from death.

But others trusted God and were tortured, preferring to die rather than turn from God and be free. They placed their hope in the resurrection to a better life. Some were mocked, and their backs were cut open with whips. Others were chained in dungeons. Some died by stoning, and some were sawed in half; others were killed with the sword. Some went about in skins of sheep and goats, hungry and oppressed and mistreated. They were too good for this world. They wandered over deserts and mountains, hiding in caves and holes in the ground.

All of these people we have mentioned received God's approval because of their faith, yet none of them received all that God had promised. For God had far better things in mind for us that would also benefit them, for they can't receive the prize at the end of the race until we finish the race." (NLT)

DAY 15

CONTENT WITH . . . WHATEVER

*Main Point: One eventual result of spiritual growth
is contentment with whatever God provides.*

I rejoiced greatly in the Lord that at last you re-
newed your concern for me.Indeed, you were
concerned, but you had no opportunity to show it. I
am not saying this because I am in need, for I have
learned to be content whatever the circumstances. I
know what it is to be in need, and I know what it
is to have plenty. I have learned the secret of being
content in any and every situation, whether well fed
or hungry, whether living in plenty or in want. I
can do all this through him who gives me strength.

—*Philippians 4:10-13*

*TODAY'S QUESTION: WHAT DO YOU
THINK IT MEANS TO BE CONTENT?*

READ ALSO: 1 TIMOTHY 6:6-10

ADDITIONAL READING

2 CORINTHIANS 12:7-10

Therefore, so that I would not become arrogant, a thorn in the flesh was given to me, a messenger of Satan to trouble me—so that I would not become arrogant. I asked the Lord three times about this, that it would depart from me. But he said to me, "My grace is enough for you, for my power is made perfect in weakness." So then, I will boast most gladly about my weaknesses, so that the power of Christ may reside in me. Therefore I am content with weaknesses, with insults, with troubles, with persecutions and difficulties for the sake of Christ, for whenever I am weak, then I am strong. (Net Bible)

MY GRACE IS ENOUGH FOR
YOU, FOR MY POWER IS MADE
PERFECT IN WEAKNESS

DAY 16

WASTED EFFORT?

Main Point: No amount of human effort replaces faith and dependence on God.

For it is by grace you have been saved, through faith—and this is not from yourselves, it is the gift of God— not by works, so that no one can boast. For we are God's handiwork, created in Christ Jesus to do good works, which God prepared in advance for us to do.

—Ephesians 2:8-10

TODAY'S QUESTION: WHAT CAN THESE VERSES TEACH US ABOUT SALVATION?

READ ALSO: PSALMS 127:1-2

ADDITIONAL READING

JOHN 7:38-39

Whoever believes in me, as the Scripture has said, 'Out of his heart will flow rivers of living water.' Now this he said about the Spirit, whom those who believed in him were to receive, for as yet the Spirit had not been given, because Jesus was not yet glorified. (ESV)

JOHN 20:24-31

Now Thomas, one of the Twelve, called the Twin, was not with them when Jesus came. So the other disciples told him, "We have seen the Lord." But he said to them, "Unless I see in his hands the mark of the nails, and place my finger into the mark of the nails, and place my hand into his side, I will never believe."

Eight days later, his disciples were inside again, and Thomas was with them. Although the doors were locked, Jesus came and stood among them and said, "Peace be with you." Then he said to Thomas, "Put your finger here, and see my hands; and put out your hand, and place it in my side. Do not disbelieve, but believe." Thomas answered him, "My Lord and my God!" Jesus said to him, "Have you believed because you have seen me? Blessed are those who have not seen and yet have believed."

Now Jesus did many other signs in the presence of the disciples, which are not written in this book; but these are written so that you may believe that Jesus is the Christ, the Son of God, and that by believing you may have life in his name." (ESV)

DAY 17

THE GREATEST OF THESE

Main Point: We are challenged to show a much more genuine and effective love for others.

Love is patient, love is kind. It does not envy, it does not boast, it is not proud. It does not dishonor others, it is not self-seeking, it is not easily angered, it keeps no record of wrongs. Love does not delight in evil but rejoices with the truth. It always protects, always trusts, always hopes, always perseveres.

—*1 Corinthians 13:4-7*

TODAY'S QUESTION: IN WHAT WAYS ARE
YOU INSPIRED BY THESE VERSES?

READ ALSO: JOHN 13:35

ADDITIONAL READING

GALATIANS 5:13-26

For you were called to freedom, brothers and sisters; only do not use your freedom as an opportunity to indulge your flesh, but through love serve one another. For the whole law can be summed up in a single commandment, namely, "You must love your neighbor as yourself." However, if you continually bite and devour one another, beware that you are not consumed by one another. But I say, live by the Spirit and you will not carry out the desires of the flesh. For the flesh has desires that are opposed to the Spirit, and the Spirit has desires that are opposed to the flesh, for these are in opposition to each other, so that you cannot do what you want. But if you are led by the Spirit, you are not under the law. Now the works of the flesh are obvious: sexual immorality, impurity, depravity, idolatry, sorcery, hostilities, strife, jealousy, outbursts of anger, selfish rivalries, dissensions, factions, envying, murder, drunkenness, carousing, and similar things. I am warning you, as I had warned you before: Those who practice such things will not inherit the kingdom of God!

But the fruit of the Spirit is love, joy, peace, patience, kindness, goodness, faithfulness, gentleness, and self-control. Against such things there is no law. Now those who belong to Christ have crucified the flesh with its passions and desires. If we live by the Spirit, let us also behave in accordance with the Spirit. Let us not become conceited, provoking one another, being jealous of one another. (NET Bible)

DAY 18

GET BACK ON THAT ALTAR

Main Point: We no longer sacrifice animals to God; we sacrifice ourselves.

Therefore, I urge you, brothers and sisters, in view of God's mercy, to offer your bodies as a living sacrifice, holy and pleasing to God—this is your true and proper worship. Do not conform to the pattern of this world, but be transformed by the renewing of your mind. Then you will be able to test and approve what God's will is—his good, pleasing and perfect will.

—*Romans 12:1-2*

TODAY'S QUESTION: *WHAT DO YOU THINK IT MEANS TO BE A LIVING SACRIFICE?*

READ ALSO: HEBREWS 13:15-16

ADDITIONAL READING

GALATIANS 3:1-14

You stupid people of Galatia! Who put you under an evil spell? Wasn't Christ Jesus' crucifixion clearly described to you? I want to learn only one thing from you. Did you receive the Spirit by your own efforts to live according to a set of standards or by believing what you heard? Are you that stupid? Did you begin in a spiritual way only to end up doing things in a human way? Did you suffer so much for nothing? {I doubt} that it was for nothing! Does God supply you with the Spirit and work miracles among you through your own efforts or through believing what you heard?

Abraham serves as an example. He believed God, and that faith was regarded by God to be his approval of Abraham. You must understand that people who have faith are Abraham's descendants. Scripture saw ahead of time that God would give his approval to non-Jewish people who have faith. So Scripture announced the Good News to Abraham ahead of time when it said, "Through you all the people of the world will be blessed." So people who believe are blessed together with Abraham, the man of faith.

Certainly, there is a curse on all who rely on their own efforts to live according to a set of standards because Scripture says, "Whoever doesn't obey everything that is written in Moses' Teachings is cursed." No one receives God's approval by obeying the law's standards since, "The person who has God's approval will live by faith." Laws have nothing to do with faith, but, "Whoever obeys laws will live because of the laws he obeys."

Christ paid the price to free us from the curse that God's laws bring by becoming cursed instead of us. Scripture says, "Everyone who is hung on a tree is cursed." {Christ paid the price} so that the blessing promised to Abraham would come to all the people of the world through Jesus Christ and we would receive the promised Spirit through faith." (GWT)

16 SCRIPTURE READINGS ON SPIRITUAL GROWTH

INTRODUCTION TO BIBLE READINGS

When we study the Scriptures, we find many common themes among the captivating stories. Throughout these many themes, God incorporates the elements we need for a successful spiritual walk with Him.

The last part of this book captures 16 scripture readings that will help you aid your spiritual growth, deepen your faith, and intensify your daily time spent in the Word. As you read these selections, you'll discover God's patience, His provision, and His providence.

Invest a few minutes each day with this book. You'll find that after a month, you've grown in your personal relationship with Him and are daily pursuing a closer walk with Him.

These passages are reprinted in their entirety but without commentary in hopes that you will enjoy reflective, undistracted moments with God's Word.

Be a Bible People! Read the Word!

READING 1 | FAITH: TRUSTING GOD WITH EVERYTHING

GENESIS 22:1-14

Some time later God tested Abraham. He said to him, "Abraham!"

"Here I am," he replied.

Then God said, "Take your son, your only son, Isaac, whom you love, and go to the region of Moriah. Sacrifice him there as a burnt offering on one of the mountains I will tell you about."

Early the next morning Abraham got up and saddled his donkey. He took with him two of his servants and his son Isaac. When he had cut enough wood for the burnt offering, he set out for the place God had told him about. On the third day Abraham looked up and saw the place in the distance. He said to his servants, "Stay here with the donkey while I and the boy go over there. We will worship and then we will come back to you."

Abraham took the wood for the burnt offering and placed it on his son Isaac, and he
himself carried the fire and the knife. As the
two of them went on together, Isaac spoke up
and said to his father Abraham, "Father?"

"Yes, my son?" Abraham replied.

"The fire and wood are here," Isaac said, "but
where is the lamb for the burnt offering?"

Abraham answered, "God himself will provide the lamb for the burnt offering, my son."
And the two of them went on together.

When they reached the place God had told
him about, Abraham built an altar there and ar-
ranged the wood on it. He bound his son Isaac
and laid him on the altar, on top of the wood.
Then he reached out his hand and took the knife
to slay his son. But the angel of the Lord called
out to him from heaven, "Abraham! Abraham!"

"Here I am," he replied.

"Do not lay a hand on the boy," he said.
"Do not do anything to him. Now I know that

you fear God, because you have not with-
held from me your son, your only son."

Abraham looked up and there in a thicket he saw
a ram caught by its horns. He went over and took
the ram and sacrificed it as a burnt offering instead
of his son. So Abraham called that place The Lord
Will Provide. And to this day it is said, "On the
mountain of the Lord it will be provided." (NIV)

Reading 2 | Faith: Trusting God through Prayer

I SAMUEL 1:7-20

Year after year it was the same—Peninnah would taunt Hannah as they went to the Tabernacle. Hannah would finally be reduced to tears and would not even eat.

"What's the matter, Hannah?" Elkanah would ask. "Why aren't you eating? Why be so sad just because you have no children? You have me—isn't that better than having ten sons?"

Once when they were at Shiloh, Hannah went over to the Tabernacle after supper to pray to the Lord. Eli the priest was sitting at his customary place beside the entrance. Hannah was in deep anguish, crying bitterly as she prayed to the Lord. And she made this vow: "O Lord Almighty, if you will look down upon my sorrow and answer my prayer and give me a son, then

I will give him back to you. He will be yours for his entire lifetime, and as a sign that he has been dedicated to the Lord, his hair will never be cut."

As she was praying to the Lord, Eli watched her. Seeing her lips moving but hearing no sound, he thought she had been drinking. "Must you come here drunk?" he demanded. "Throw away your wine!"

"Oh no, sir!" she replied, "I'm not drunk! But I am very sad, and I was pouring out my heart to the Lord. Please don't think I am a wicked woman! For I have been praying out of great anguish and sorrow."

"In that case," Eli said, "cheer up! May the God of Israel grant the request you have asked of him."

"Oh, thank you, sir!" she exclaimed. Then she went back and began to eat again, and she was no longer sad.

The entire family got up early the next morning and went to worship the Lord once more. Then they returned home to Ramah. When Elkanah slept with Hannah, the Lord remembered her request, and in due time she gave birth to a son. She named him Samuel, for she said, "I asked the Lord for him." (NLT)

Reading 3 | Faith: Trusting God for Protection

2 Chronicles 20:20-30

And they rose early in the morning and went out into the wilderness of Tekoa. And when they went out, Jehoshaphat stood and said, "Hear me, Judah and inhabitants of Jerusalem! Believe in the Lord your God, and you will be established; believe his prophets, and you will succeed." And when he had taken counsel with the people, he appointed those who were to sing to the Lord and praise him in holy attire, as they went before the army, and say,

"Give thanks to the Lord,

for his steadfast love endures forever."

And when they began to sing and praise, the Lord set an ambush against the men of Ammon, Moab, and Mount Seir, who had come against Judah, so that they were routed. For the men of Ammon and Moab rose against the inhabitants

of Mount Seir, devoting them to destruction, and
when they had made an end of the inhabitants
of Seir, they all helped to destroy one another.

When Judah came to the watchtower of the wilderness, they looked toward the horde, and behold,
there were dead bodies lying on the ground; none
had escaped. When Jehoshaphat and his people
came to take their spoil, they found among them,
in great numbers, goods, clothing, and precious
things, which they took for themselves until they
could carry no more. They were three days in
taking the spoil, it was so much. On the fourth day
they assembled in the Valley of Beracah, for there
they blessed the Lord. Therefore the name of that
place has been called the Valley of Beracah to this
day. Then they returned, every man of Judah and
Jerusalem, and Jehoshaphat at their head, return-
ing to Jerusalem with joy, for the Lord had made
them rejoice over their enemies. They came to
Jerusalem with harps and lyres and trumpets, to
the house of the Lord. And the fear of God came
on all the kingdoms of the countries when they
heard that the Lord had fought against the enemies

of Israel. So the realm of Jehoshaphat was quiet, for his God gave him rest all around." (ESV)

READING 4 | FAITH IN HIS POWER

MATTHEW 8:1-3

When Jesus came down from the mountain, large
crowds followed him.   A man with a serious skin
disease came and bowed down in front of him. The
man said to Jesus, "Sir, if you're willing, you can
make me clean."   Jesus reached out, touched him,
and said, "I'm willing. So be clean!" Immediately, his
skin disease went away, and he was clean. (GWT)

MATTHEW 8:5-13

When Jesus went to Capernaum, a Ro-
man army officer came to beg him for help.
The officer said, "Sir, my servant is lying at
home paralyzed and in terrible pain."

Jesus said to him, "I'll come to heal him."

The officer responded, "Sir, I don't deserve
to have you come into my house. But just give a
command, and my servant will be healed. As you
know, I'm in a chain of command and have sol-
diers at my command. I tell one of them, 'Go!'

and he goes, and another, 'Come!' and he comes. I tell my servant, 'Do this!' and he does it."

Jesus was amazed when he heard this. He said to those who were following him, "I can guarantee this truth: I haven't found faith as great as this in anyone in Israel. I can guarantee that many will come from all over the world. They will eat with Abraham, Isaac, and Jacob in the kingdom of heaven. The citizens of that kingdom will be thrown outside into the darkness. People will cry and be in extreme pain there.

Jesus told the officer, "Go! What you believed will be done for you." And at that moment the servant was healed. (GWT)

MATTHEW 9:18-31

A {synagogue} leader came to Jesus while he was talking to John's disciples. He bowed down in front of Jesus and said, "My daughter just died. Come, lay your hand on her, and she will live."

Jesus and his disciples got up and followed the man.

Then a woman came up behind Jesus and touched the edge of his clothes. She had been suffering from chronic bleeding for twelve years. She thought, "If I only touch his clothes, I'll get well."

When Jesus turned and saw her he said, "Cheer up, daughter! Your faith has made you well." At that very moment the woman became well.

Jesus came to the {synagogue} leader's house. He saw flute players and a noisy crowd. He said to them, "Leave! The girl is not dead. She's sleeping." But they laughed at him.

When the crowd had been put outside, Jesus went in, took her hand, and the girl came back to life.

The news about this spread throughout that region.

When Jesus left that place, two blind men followed him. They shouted, "Have mercy on us, Son of David."

Jesus went into a house, and the blind men followed him. He said to them, "Do you believe that I can do this?"

"Yes, Lord," they answered.

He touched their eyes and said, "What you have believed will be done for you!" Then they could see.

He warned them, "Don't let anyone know about this!" But they went out and spread the news about him throughout that region. (GWT)

READING 5 | FAITH IN HIS TOUCH

MATTHEW 14:34-36

When they had crossed over, they came to land
at Gennesaret. And when the men of that place
recognized Him, they sent word into all that sur-
rounding district and brought to Him all who
were sick; and they implored Him that they
might just touch the fringe of His cloak; and
as many as touched it were cured." (NASB)

MATTHEW 15:21-28

Jesus went away from there, and withdrew into the
district of Tyre and Sidon. And a Canaanite woman
from that region came out and began to cry out,
saying, "Have mercy on me, Lord, Son of David; my
daughter is cruelly demon-possessed." But He did
not answer her a word. And His disciples came and
implored Him, saying, "Send her away, because she
keeps shouting at us." But He answered and said, "I
was sent only to the lost sheep of the house of Israel."
But she came and began to bow down before Him,
saying, "Lord, help me!" And He answered and said,

"It is not good to take the children's bread and throw it to the dogs." But she said, "Yes, Lord; but even the dogs feed on the crumbs which fall from their masters' table." Then Jesus said to her, "O woman, your faith is great; it shall be done for you as you wish." And her daughter was healed at once. " (NASB)

READING 6 | FAITH IN ACTION

MATTHEW 21:18-22

Early in the morning, as he was on his way back to the city, he was hungry. Seeing a fig tree by the road, he went up to it but found nothing on it except leaves. Then he said to it, "May you never bear fruit again!" Immediately the tree withered.

When the disciples saw this, they were amazed. "How did the fig tree wither so quickly?" they asked.

Jesus replied, "I tell you the truth, if you have faith and do not doubt, not only can you do what was done to the fig tree, but also you can say to this mountain, 'Go, throw yourself into the sea,' and it will be done. If you believe, you will receive whatever you ask for in prayer." (NIV)

MATTHEW 17:14-20

When they came to the crowd, a man came up to Jesus, falling on his knees before Him and saying, "Lord, have mercy on my son, for he is a lunatic and is very ill; for he often falls into the fire and often into the water. "I brought him to Your disciples, and they could not cure him." And Jesus answered and said, "You unbelieving and perverted generation, how long shall I be with you? How long shall I put up with you? Bring him here to Me." And Jesus rebuked him, and the demon came out of him, and the boy was cured at once.

Then the disciples came to Jesus privately and said, "Why could we not drive it out?" And He said to them, "Because of the littleness of your faith; for truly I say to you, if you have faith the size of a mustard seed, you will say to this mountain, 'Move from here to there,' and it will move; and nothing will be impossible to you. " (NASB)

MARK 5:21-43

When Jesus had again crossed over by boat to the other side of the lake, a large crowd gathered around him while he was by the lake. Then one of the synagogue rulers, named Jairus, came there. Seeing Jesus, he fell at his feet and pleaded earnestly with him, "My little daughter is dying. Please come and put your hands on her so that she will be healed and live." So Jesus went with him.

A large crowd followed and pressed around him. And a woman was there who had been subject to bleeding for twelve years. She had suffered a great deal under the care of many doctors and had spent all she had, yet instead of getting better she grew worse. When she heard about Jesus, she came up behind him in the crowd and touched his cloak, because she thought, "If I just touch his clothes, I will be healed." Immediately her bleeding stopped and she felt in her body that she was freed from her suffering.

At once Jesus realized that power had gone out from him. He turned around in the crowd and asked, "Who touched my clothes?"

"You see the people crowding against you," his disciples answered, "and yet you can ask, 'Who touched me?' "

But Jesus kept looking around to see who had done it. Then the woman, knowing what had happened to her, came and fell at his feet and, trembling with fear, told him the whole truth. He said to her, "Daughter, your faith has healed you.

Go in peace and be freed from your suffering."

While Jesus was still speaking, some men came from the house of Jairus, the synagogue ruler. "Your daughter is dead," they said. "Why bother the teacher any more?"

Ignoring what they said, Jesus told the synagogue ruler, "Don't be afraid; just believe."

He did not let anyone follow him except Peter, James and John the brother of James. When they came to the home of the synagogue ruler, Jesus saw a commotion, with people crying and wailing loudly. He went in and said to them, "Why all this commotion and wailing? The child is not dead but asleep." But they laughed at him.

After he put them all out, he took the child's father and mother and the disciples who were with him, and went in where the child was. He took her by the hand and said to her, "Talitha koum!" (which means, "Little girl, I say to you, get up!"). Immediately the girl stood up and walked around (she was twelve years old). At this they were completely astonished. He gave strict orders not to let anyone know about this, and told them to give her something to eat. (NIV)

READING 7 | FAITH IS INTENTIONAL

ROMANS 10:17-21

So faith comes from what is heard, and what is heard comes through the word of Christ. But I ask, have they not heard? Indeed they have; for their voice has gone out to all the earth, and their words to the ends of the world. Again I ask, did Israel not understand? First Moses says, "I will make you jealous of those who are not a nation; with a foolish nation I will make you angry." Then Isaiah is so bold as to say, "I have been found by those who did not seek me; I have shown myself to those who did not ask for me." But of Israel he says, "All day long I have held out my hands to a disobedient and contrary people." (NRSV)

ROMANS 14:19-23

Let us then pursue what makes for peace and for mutual upbuilding. Do not, for the sake of food, destroy the work of God. Everything is indeed clean, but it is wrong for you to make others fall by what you eat; it is good not to eat meat or drink wine or do anything that makes your brother or sister stumble. The faith that you have, have as your own conviction before God. Blessed are those who have no reason to condemn themselves because of what they approve. But those who have doubts are condemned if they eat, because they do not act from faith; for whatever does not proceed from faith is sin." (NRSV)

2 CORINTHIANS 5:6-7
So we are always confident; even though we know that while we are at home in the body we are away from the Lord-- for we walk by faith, not by sight." (NRSV)

Reading 8 | Faith Drives Good Works

JAMES 2:14-26

What good is it, my brothers, if someone says he has faith but does not have works? Can that faith save him? If a brother or sister is poorly clothed and lacking in daily food, and one of you says to them, "Go in peace, be warmed and filled," without giving them the things needed for the body, what good is that? So also faith by itself, if it does not have works, is dead.

But someone will say, "You have faith and I have works." Show me your faith apart from your works, and I will show you my faith by my works. You believe that God is one; you do well. Even the demons believe—and shudder! Do you want to be shown, you foolish person, that faith apart from works is useless? Was not Abraham our father justified by works when he offered up his son Isaac on the altar? You see that faith was active along with his works, and faith was completed by his works; and the Scripture was fulfilled that says, "Abraham believed God, and it was counted to him as righteousness"— and he was called a friend of God. You see that a person is justified by works and not by faith alone. And in the same way was not also Rahab the prostitute justified by works when she received the messengers and sent them out by another way? For as the body apart from the spirit is dead, so also faith apart from works is dead." (ESV)

READING 9 | FAITH IN THE SPIRIT

I JOHN 3:21-24

Beloved, if our hearts do not condemn us, we
have boldness before God; and we receive from
him whatever we ask, because we obey his
commandments and do what pleases him.

And this is his commandment, that we should
believe in the name of his Son Jesus Christ and
love one another, just as he has commanded us. All
who obey his commandments abide in him, and he
abides in them. And by this we know that he abides
in us, by the Spirit that he has given us." (NRSV)

JOHN 15:26-16:15

"When the Advocate comes, whom I will send
to you from the Father—the Spirit of truth
who goes out from the Father—he will testify about me. 27 And you also must testify, for
you have been with me from the beginning.

"All this I have told you so that you will not fall
away. They will put you out of the synagogue; in

fact, the time is coming when anyone who kills you will think they are offering a service to God. They will do such things because they have not known the Father or me. I have told you this, so that when their time comes you will remember that I warned you about them. I did not tell you this from the beginning because I was with you, but now I am going to him who sent me. None of you asks me, 'Where are you going?' Rather, you are filled with grief because I have said these things. But very truly I tell you, it is for your good that I am going away. Unless I go away, the Advocate will not come to you; but if I go, I will send him to you. When he comes, he will prove the world to be in the wrong about sin and righteousness and judgment: about sin, because people do not believe in me; about righteousness, because I am going to the Father, where you can see me no longer; and about judgment, because the prince of this world now stands condemned.

"I have much more to say to you, more than you can now bear. But when he, the Spirit of truth, comes, he will guide you into all the truth.

He will not speak on his own; he will speak only what he hears, and he will tell you what is yet to come.   He will glorify me because it is from me that he will receive what he will make known to you.   All that belongs to the Father is mine. That is why I said the Spirit will receive from me what he will make known to you."

READING 10
OBEDIENCE TRIUMPHS
OVER SACRIFICE

I SAMUEL 15:12-23

Early the next morning Samuel went to find Saul. Someone told him, "Saul went to the town of Carmel to set up a monument to himself; then he went on to Gilgal."

When Samuel finally found him, Saul greeted him cheerfully. "May the Lord bless you," he said. "I have carried out the Lord's command!"

"Then what is all the bleating of sheep and goats and the lowing of cattle I hear?" Samuel demanded.

"It's true that the army spared the best of the sheep, goats, and cattle," Saul admitted. "But they are going to sacrifice them to the Lord your God. We have destroyed everything else."

Then Samuel said to Saul, "Stop! Listen to what the Lord told me last night!"

"What did he tell you?" Saul asked.

And Samuel told him, "Although you may think little of yourself, are you not the leader of the tribes of Israel? The Lord has anointed you king of Israel. And the Lord sent you on a mission and told you, 'Go and completely destroy the sinners, the Amalekites, until they are all dead.' Why haven't you obeyed the Lord? Why did you rush for the plunder and do what was evil in the Lord's sight?"

"But I did obey the Lord," Saul insisted. "I carried out the mission he gave me. I brought back King Agag, but I destroyed everyone else. Then my troops brought in the best of the sheep, goats, cattle, and plunder to sacrifice to the Lord your God in Gilgal."

But Samuel replied,

"What is more pleasing to the Lord: your burnt offerings and sacrifices or your obedience to his voice? Listen! Obedience is better than sacrifice, and submission is better than offering the fat of rams. Rebellion is as sinful as witchcraft, and stubbornness as bad as worshiping idols. So because you have rejected the command of the Lord, he has rejected you as king." (NLT)

READING 11
OBEDIENCE
HONORS HIS
HOLINESS

PSALM 119:1-10

Happy are people of integrity,

who follow the law of the Lord.

Happy are those who obey his decrees

and search for him with all their hearts.

They do not compromise with evil,

and they walk only in his paths.

You have charged us

to keep your commandments carefully.

Oh, that my actions would consistently

reflect your principles!

Then I will not be disgraced

when I compare my life with your commands.

When I learn your righteous laws,

I will thank you by living as I should!

I will obey your principles.

Please don't give up on me!

How can a young person stay pure?

By obeying your word and following its rules.

I have tried my best to find you—

don't let me wander from
your commands." (NLT)

READING 12
OBEDIENCE YIELDS
BLESSINGS

PSALM 119:56-62

This blessing has fallen to me,

    that I have kept your precepts.

The Lord is my portion;

    I promise to keep your words.

I entreat your favor with all my heart;

    be gracious to me according to your promise.

When I think on my ways,

    I turn my feet to your testimonies;

I hasten and do not delay

    to keep your commandments.

Though the cords of the wicked ensnare me,

    I do not forget your law.

At midnight I rise to praise you,

because of your righteous rules." (ESV)

JAMES 2:10-13

For whoever keeps the whole law and yet stumbles at just one point is guilty of breaking all of it. For he who said, "Do not commit adultery," also said, "Do not murder." If you do not commit adultery but do commit murder, you have become a lawbreaker.

Speak and act as those who are going to be judged by the law that gives freedom, because judgment without mercy will be shown to anyone who has not been merciful. Mercy triumphs over judgment!" (NIV)

Reading 13
Obedience, because of His Deliverance

ROMANS 6:17-18

But thanks be to God that you, having once been slaves of sin, have become obedient from the heart to the form of teaching to which you were entrusted, and that you, having been set free from sin, have become slaves of righteousness." (NRSV)

JOSHUA 22:1-5

Then Joshua summoned the Reubenites, the Gadites, and the half-tribe of Manasseh, and said to them, "You have observed all that Moses the servant of the Lord commanded you, and have obeyed me in all that I have commanded you; you have not forsaken your kindred these many days, down to this day, but have been careful to keep the charge of the Lord your God. And now the Lord your God has given rest to your kindred, as he promised them; therefore turn and go to your tents in the land where your possession lies, which Moses the servant of the Lord gave you on the other side of the Jordan. Take good care to observe the commandment and instruction that Moses the servant of the Lord commanded you, to love the Lord your God, to walk in all his ways, to keep his commandments, and to hold fast to him, and to serve him with all your heart and with all your soul."

Reading 14
Obedience To the
One Who Sustains

JOHN 15:1-17

{Then Jesus said,} "I am the true vine, and my Father takes care of the vineyard. He removes every one of my branches that doesn't produce fruit. He also prunes every branch that does produce fruit to make it produce more fruit.

"You are already clean because of what I have told you. Live in me, and I will live in you. A branch cannot produce any fruit by itself. It has to stay attached to the vine. In the same way, you cannot produce fruit unless you live in me.

"I am the vine. You are the branches. Those who live in me while I live in them will produce a lot of fruit. But you can't produce anything without me. Whoever doesn't live in me is thrown away like a branch and dries up. Branches like this are gathered, thrown into a fire, and burned. If you live in me and what I say lives in you, then ask for anything you want, and it will be yours. You give glory to my Father when you produce a lot of fruit and therefore show that you are my disciples.

"I have loved you the same way the Father has loved me. So live in my love. If you obey my commandments, you will live in my love. I have obeyed my Father's commandments, and in that way I live in his love. I have told you this so that you will be as joyful as I am, and your joy will be complete. Love each other as I have loved you. This is what I'm commanding you to do. The greatest love you can show is to give your life for your friends. You are my friends if you obey my commandments. I don't call you servants anymore, because a servant doesn't know what his master is doing. But I've called you friends because I've made known to you everything that I've heard from my Father. You didn't choose me, but I chose you. I have appointed you to go, to produce fruit that will last, and to ask the Father in my name to give you whatever you ask for. Love each other. This is what I'm commanding you to do. (GWT)

READING 15
OBEDIENCE BRINGS STRENGTH

LUKE 6:46-49

"Why do you call Me, 'Lord, Lord,' and do not do what I say? "Everyone who comes to Me and hears My words and acts on them, I will show you whom he is like: he is like a man building a house, who dug deep and laid a foundation on the rock; and when a flood occurred, the torrent burst against that house and could not shake it, because it had been well built. "But the one who has heard and has not acted accordingly, is like a man who built a house on the ground without any foundation; and the torrent burst against it and immediately it collapsed, and the ruin of that house was great." (NASB)

ACTS 4:18-21

And when they had summoned them, they commanded them not to speak or teach at all in the name of Jesus. But Peter and John answered and said to them, "Whether it is right in the sight of God to give heed to you rather than to God, you be the judge; for we cannot stop speaking about what we have seen and heard." When they had threatened them further, they let them go (finding no basis on which to punish them) on account of the people, because they were all glorifying God for what had happened;" (NASB)

READING 16
OBEDIENCE
WITHOUT QUESTION

GENESIS 12:1-4

Then the Lord told Abram, "Leave your country, your relatives, and your father's house, and go to the land that I will show you. I will cause you to become the father of a great nation. I will bless you and make you famous, and I will make you a blessing to others. I will bless those who bless you and curse those who curse you. All the families of the earth will be blessed through you."

So Abram departed as the Lord had instructed him, and Lot went with him. Abram was seventy-five years old when he left Haran. (NLT)

DEUTERONOMY 11:1-15

Love the LORD your God and keep his requirements, his decrees, his laws and his commands always. ...

Observe therefore all the commands I am giving you today, so that you may have the strength to go in and take over the land that you are crossing the Jordan to possess, and so that you may live long in the land that the LORD swore to your forefathers to give to them and their descendants, a land flowing with milk and honey. ...

So if you faithfully obey the commands I am giving you today – to love the LORD your God and to serve him will all your heart and with all your soul –then I will send rain on your land in its season, both autumn and spring rains, so that you may gather in your grain, new wine and oil. I will provide grass in the fields for your cattle, and you will eat and be satisfied. (NIV)

FOLLOWING JESUS DEVOTIONAL BOOK

"Come, follow me." With those three simple words, Jesus called his first disciples to join him on a journey that would forever change their lives. Today, he offers you the same invitation. But what does it really mean to follow Jesus?

Following Jesus Daily Devotional takes you through Scripture toward refreshment and a deeper understanding of what it means to walk every step with Jesus. Each of the 100 daily readings provides a short devotion, a key Bible verse, a reflection question, and a prayer. With this faith-building devotional, you will not only cover topics that apply to your daily living, such as overcoming fear and discovering hope; but you will also strengthen the very foundation of your faith by covering key discipleship topics, including the basics of salvation, Bible reading, church, fruit of the Spirit, witnessing, and more.

Learn more at www.bit.ly/FollowingJesusDevo

Made in the USA
Lexington, KY
02 April 2018